Freddie Starr, born Frederick Leslie Fo
Huyton, Lancashire England, UK, was a
singer and actor. Starr was the lead si
group the Midniters during the early '60s, before becoming
famous during the early '70s following his appearances on
Opportunity Knocks and the Royal Variety Performance. He
starred on several TV shows in the '90s, including Freddie Starr
(1993–94), The Freddie Starr Show (1996–98) and An Audience
with Freddie Starr during 1996. He presented the game show
Beat the Crusher in 1999, before appearing as a contestant on
the TV show I'm a Celebrity...Get Me Out of Here! in 2011.

Freddie was one of 7 children, his twin brother having died at
birth. His father was a bricklayer and bare-knuckled boxer, who
was often unemployed, while his mother Hilda (née Bradford)
was a German Jew. As a young child he was repeatedly beaten
by his father when he was drunk, once breaking both of his
son's legs. At the age of 6, Starr stopped speaking then was
taken into care, becoming a lifelong teetotaler. Freddie stated in
his 2001 autobiography Unwrapped, that speech problems were
reason that he spent two years away from home as a child. He
attended Sylvester's Primary, followed by Huyton Secondary
Modern, his father having died when Starr was in his early
teens.

Freddie was encouraged by his mother to perform in working
mens clubs and pubs from the age of 12 and was a member of
the Hilda Fallon Roadshow for 5 years, which toured community
halls and hospitals. He appeared as a teenager in the film
Violent Playground (1958), credited under his birth name. Starr
was the lead singer of the Merseybeat pop band The Midniters
or Midnighters during the early '60s, which was managed by
Brian Epstein. The group recorded 3 singles, produced by Joe

Meek, all failing to enter the charts, despite performing in Hamburg's nightclubs at around the same time as the Beatles.

When till almost unknown to TV audiences, Freddie was "discovered" by the talent show, Opportunity Knocks in 1967, on which he appeared as part of comedy/beat act Freddie Starr and the Delmonts, winning the popular vote each time for 6 weeks. Starr appeared on the Royal Variety Performance during 1970, having impersonated Mick Jagger of the Rolling Stones and Adolf Hitler in Wellington Boots. Freddie also impersonated Elvis Presley and Ray Charles during his career, having had a chart album titled After the Laughter then a UK Top 10 single, "It's You", during March 1974.

Starr was one of the main performers on the TV series Who Do You Do? (1972), then a regular on the TV panel show Jokers Wild. A first attempt at his own series, Ready Freddie Starr (1974), was cut to a single special programme because he got involved in disputes with the production team at London Weekend Television (LWT), before landing his own BBC series in 1976.

Mark Lawson wrote that Freddie's wit, "relied on broad punchlines and silly slapstick", while Stuart Jeffries in his Guardian obituary wrote that his act was "pre-cerebral, unrepentantly sexist, often racist comedy that was rendered overwhelmingly obsolete by the late '80s". Starr developed an addiction to Valium which lasted for 20 years, from 1974. The chat show host Michael Parkinson wrote that it "addled his talent and confused his personality", eroding "a virtuosity equalled by only a very few entertainers".

Freddie was the subject of one of the most infamous British tabloid newspaper headlines, The Sun having had: "Freddie

Starr Ate My Hamster" as its main headline. The story stated that Starr had been staying at the home of Vince McCaffrey and his 23-year-old girlfriend Lea La Salle in Birchwood, Cheshire, when the alleged incident took place.

Freddie was alleged to have returned home from a performance at a Manchester nightclub during the early hours of the morning, demanding that La Salle make him a sandwich. When she refused, he was accused of having gone into the kitchen then put her pet hamster Supersonic between two slices of bread, before proceeding to eat it.

Starr gave his own account of the story in his autobiography Unwrapped (2001), stating that the only time he'd ever stayed at Vince McCaffrey's house was in 1979, and that the alleged incident was a complete fabrication. Freddie wrote in his book: "I've never eaten or even nibbled a live hamster, gerbil, guinea pig, mouse, shrew, vole or any other small mammal".

At first the story had no effect on Starr's career, tickets for a forthcoming tour having been selling slowly but after the headline in The Sun, the publicity led to the addition of 12 dates to his itinerary, boosting his fee by £1 million. The man behind the hamster story was the British publicist Max Clifford then Freddie's agent, who invented it as a practical joke.

When Clifford was asked in a TV interview with Esther Rantzen some years later whether Starr really had eaten a hamster, his reply was "Of course not" but was unapologetic, insisting that the story had given a huge boost to Starr's career. The BBC nominated "Freddie Starr Ate My Hamster" during May 2006, as one of the best known British newspaper headlines over the past century.

Freddie's frustration at being perpetually linked to the hamster story was expressed in a newspaper interview, when he stated: "I'm fed up of people shouting out 'Did you eat that hamster, Freddie?' Now I say, give me £1 and I'll tell you. Then if they give me £1, I say 'No' and walk away." He said that the story arose after he made an offhand joke about eating a hamster in a sandwich. The Sun's front page headline after his death on 9th May 2019 was "Freddie Starr Joins His Hamster". Starr was a vegetarian from his teens onwards.

He appeared in Freddie Starr (1993–94) then The Freddie Starr Show (1996–98) made by Central. At the beginning of his appearance on LWT's An Audience with Freddie Starr in 1996, he threw handfuls of live maggots at the audience, but Another Audience with Freddie Starr followed during 1997, when he hit eggs with a golf club into the audience.

Freddie was the owner of Miinnehoma, the winning horse in the Grand National race of 1994. He wasn't present on the day because of TV commitments elsewhere, but gave an unusual post-race interview live on TV to presenter Des Lynam via a mobile phone, with the viewers only able to hear Lynam's responses to what Starr was saying.

He appeared in Living with the Dead in March 2009, a reality TV show about people being haunted by ghosts, Freddie having claimed his 1930s house was being haunted by an evil entity which he called George. During the show it appeared that he was possessed by this entity, it later being revealed that the entity's name was Roger. During the episode, Starr said that he'd always been spiritual, having firmly believed in ghosts since he was a boy.

Freddie was due to tour during 2010, but it was cancelled when he suffered a major heart attack in April that year, requiring quadruple heart bypass surgery. The tour dates were rescheduled for 2011 after he'd recovered. Starr took part in that year's series of I'm a Celebrity... Get Me Out Of Here, but withdrew for health reasons.

Starr was a keen supporter of Everton, having appeared on ITV's coverage of the buildup to the FA Cup Final of 1984 at the height of his celebrity, in which Everton beat Watford 2–0, of which Elton John was then the chairman. Freddie appeared on the lawn outside the hotel where the Everton team were staying on the morning of the game to give an impromptu comedy performance to the players, who watched from the windows of their rooms.

Robin Coxhead, a gardener employed by Starr, was charged with the alleged theft of £41,000 worth of jewellery from the comedian's home during April 1994. When questioned by police, Coxhead claimed that the jewellery had been given to him as a reward, because he'd been giving oral sex to Freddie over a period of 5 years. However, Coxhead was discredited in court when he was unable to state whether Starr's penis was circumcised or not. Coxhead was found guilty then sentenced to 15 months in prison in 1995.

Freddie obtained an injunction during October 2012 to prevent a claim being made about his personal life. The injunction was later overturned, as it was regarded as an issue involving potential defamation, which the media outlets concerned weren't planning to publish. Channel 4 News reported allegations on 8th October 2012, relating to Starr's appearance

6

on Jimmy Savile's BBC TV show Clunk Click in 1974, which he denied through his lawyer and in media interviews.

As part of Operation Yewtree, Freddie was arrested by police at his Warwickshire home on 1st November 2012, in connection with the Jimmy Savile sexual abuse scandal. He was again arrested on 3 following occasions, without any connections to Savile, the last being on 12th February 2014, Freddie having denied the claims made against him. It was reported on 6th May 2014 that the Crown Prosecution Service had decided not to bring charges against Starr in connection with the allegations, on the grounds of "insufficient evidence".

The High Court dismissed a claim for slander and libel on 10th July 2015 that Freddie had brought against the woman who'd made the allegations relating to his appearance on Clunk Click in 1974. The woman's claim was found to be true, but the case couldn't proceed because of the passage of time. Starr emigrated to Spain, but denied this was due to his legal bill, estimated at £1 million, saying he'd planned to move to Spain whatever the outcome of the court case. Freddie was found dead at his home in Mijas, on the Costa Del Sol, Spain, on 9th May 2019, aged 76. Police believe that he died of natural causes.

Further reading

Unwrapped – My Autobiography by Freddie Starr with Alan Wightman ISBN 1-85227-961-3

Bobby Davro recalled the final time he spoke to fellow comedian Freddie Starr in an emotional interview, hours after news of his death at his home in Spain broke on Thursday 9th May '19. Davro told Good Morning Britain that he "could've been one of the last people to speak to him". "I got in touch with him, I found his number and phoned him up. At first he didn't really feel like talking and called me back. He said, 'How you doing Bob' and I said, 'Alright, how are you Freddie? Would you like to meet up for a cup of tea? I'm in town,' but he said, 'No, I've not been too well'."

Bobby told hosts Kate Garraway and Ben Shephard that he "wants to remember the Freddie we all remembered" and enjoy archive footage of him as an entertainer. Shortly after the news broke, Davro paid tribute to Starr on Twitter, hailing him as "one of the greats. I've just heard that Freddie Starr has died. He was the funniest man I've ever seen. I'm so sad we've lost one of our greatest comedy talents. RIP Freddie."

Comedian Jim Davidson and Britain's Got Talent judge Amanda Holden were among those who paid tribute to Starr online. Freddie, who was at the centre of one of the best remembered headlines in history when it was claimed he "ate a hamster", appeared on I'm A Celebrity in 2011 but was forced to pull out after a Bushtucker trial. A meal of fermented egg with a camel toe, forced comic Starr to leave the show after he suffered an allergic reaction, so had to be taken to hospital. His appearance came a year after he'd had quadruple bypass surgery following a heart attack.

Ruth Langford stated that Freddie Starr was one of the more difficult guests to interview, the day after the comedian was found dead by carer Adam Miller. However, Eamonn Holmes revealed that the last time he'd bumped into the comic they had the most 'normal' conversation they'd ever had: 'The last time I saw him was at the Oxford services station on the M40,' the This Morning TV host began.

'We pulled out and I was putting petrol in my car and he was at the other side of the pump putting petrol into his... Jeep, I think he was driving and we had a bit of a conversation there. It was probably the only sensible, normal conversation I've ever had with him."Ruth chipped in: 'He was quite hard to interview, wasn't he?'

Way back on March 13 1986, 'Freddie Starr Ate My Hamster' was splashed across The Sun after Lea Le Salle accused the star of gobbling up her pet, which subsequently stuck with Fred for the rest of his career. Following Starr's death the photographer behind that iconic front page gave the inside story. Appearing on This Morning, Steve Lewis recalled shooting Freddie for the follow up, collecting an actual hamster which was rumoured to have been killed when the comedian flew the photographer to Wapping in his helicopter:

'We'd already gone off to pet shop and got our hamster. Off we went to his home in Maidenhead. There were lots of stories following our story that the hamster didn't survive the journey in the helicopter, but I can say with a clear conscience that hamster was delivered to the pet shop,' he assured. However, Steve was pretty sure that no hamster ever passed through Freddie's lips. 'It's such a good headline it would be a shame to spoil the story. I don't think he did. I think it was a publicity stunt which made a good headline.'

Bobby Davro, Lord Sugar and Jim Davidson paid tribute to comedian Freddie Starr after he was found dead in his Costa Del Sol apartment by a carer. Speaking on Good Morning Britain Bobby revealed that the star refused to leave his house to meet him before his death: "I went over to Spain to do a couple of gigs last year. Someone said he was living in that place in Spain. After seeing those pictures... I want to remember the Freddie we all knew. Rest in peace, Freddie. He was fantastic."

Just heard the news. Freddie Starr was the greatest. — Jim Davidson (@JimDOfficial) May 9, 2019

According to some news reports Freddie Star has died in Spain . If true, sad news, he was a very funny man RIP — Lord Sugar (@Lord_Sugar) May 9, 2019

So sad - Freddie Starr. An incredible and unique talent. I remember being in a tv green room with him at Elstree studios and became exhausted with laughter at his repartee. Always difficult and awkward to interview but always worth it! Loved him. — Anne Diamond (@theannediamond) May 9, 2019

Heartbroken Davro, who impersonated Starr on his Bobby Davro On The Box show in the '80s, shared: "I've just heard that Freddie Starr has died. He was the funniest man I have ever seen. I'm so sad we have lost one of our greatest comedy talents. RIP Freddie. 💔."

Paddy McGuinness tweeted the famous Sun headline "Freddie Starr ate my hamster" having added: "It was probably a euphemism? #rip #FreddieStarr."

The entertainer was one of the biggest stars of the '70s, '80s and '90s. Fans loved his wacky, wild, and unpredictable behaviour. Freddie's body was moved from his apartment to an ambulance at 8.10pm local time. Starr became a recluse after a comeback bid flopped, neighbours in the resort of Mijas telling how he'd become a shadow of his old self after being hammered with a £960,000 legal bill defending historical sex abuse charges. He was forced to sell his £700,000 UK home then moved to Spain in 2015, despite never being charged over claims he put his hand up a girl's skirt during 1974.

Chain-smoking Freddie was reduced to living in a pokey one-bedroom flat but still loved a laugh. Starr had a history of heart problems and asthma but as recently as February '19 he'd posted a wacky Facebook snap of himself with cigarettes stuck in his mouth, nose and ears. His last post just 8 days before his death read: "I'm ok, getting tired more now but otherwise I'm doing good. I just have to say thank you all from the bottom of my heart for all the kind comments and messages, it really does mean a lot, so thank you to each and everyone of you, thanks so much. Freddie."

Starr's family were touched after undertakers offered to repatriate him for free. His carer was described by locals as a foreign woman named Neely, who'd grown close to Freddie. The Merseyside-born comic, impressionist, singer and actor had a history of heart problems and asthma. Police sources said

Starr was believed to have died of natural causes. There were no suspicious circumstances.

A neighbour said: "Freddie hadn't looked well for some time and rarely ventured out". The comedian was to be buried with his mum, despite 'pauper's grave' fears. Starr was found dead at his one-bedroom Spanish home by his housekeeper, with his cause of death later being confirmed as a heart attack. It was stated that the father-of-6 would be buried with his late mother Hilda in Liverpool: "Though estranged from his children and former wives, they felt it was only right that he be reunited with his mum. Freddie adored his mum, who was the driving force behind his career".

Previously, Starr's housekeeper said she feared he'd be buried in a "pauper's grave" after stating that "Freddie had bad feelings about back home, so I think he'd want to stay here rather than try to be repatriated but I need to speak to his family to see how they feel. He felt the British people had deserted him. In the 4 years I worked for him I never saw any of his family visit him or phone him. If the family want him to have a funeral in the UK then it could be very expensive to get him there."

However, Starr's third wife Donna Such revealed that the family were meeting to discuss Freddie's funeral plans. She stated: "We're all doing our bit, but that's all I can say at the moment. When we know more we'll be in a position, we'll make that known." Donna added that the family had been trying to trace Freddie's housekeeper, saying: "She's welcome to contact us". However, the funeral arrangements could be difficult as his estranged wife Sophie Lea was the only one who could sign off plans.

The comedian's 'worried' pals said the star was unrecognisable ahead of his death, a neighbour stating that Freddie hadn't looked well in the weeks leading up to his heart attack. They'd feared for the star after he suffered with a lung condition in 2015, when a friend said: "People wouldn't recognise him now. He honestly is completely unrecognisable from even a few years ago. We're all so worried about him."

When he was a little boy, his father told him to jump from a table, promising him, "I'll catch you". Freddie jumped but his father took his arms away, so the boy fell to the floor. "He picked me up, stroked my hair then said, 'Never trust anybody in your life. Not even your own father.'" Starr included the story in his autobiography, Unwrapped (2001), but said he had a "strict but fair" upbringing in wartime Liverpool.

However, Freddie later changed his account in 2007, stating that his father had broken his legs when he was aged just 6, the culmination of physical abuse that led him to be taken into care for two years: "My father wasn't a very nice man. I don't like to speak about it at all. You put things like this in the past and try to make something of yourself."

Starr did so, becoming a very popular entertainer, winning the talent show Opportunity Knocks 6 times during the 1960s, before going on to even greater fame at the Royal Variety Performance in 1970. "Within 30 seconds I had the audience helpless with laughter," he recalled of that night, adding that he got the first encore in 47 years of the show with his impersonations of Adam Faith, Billy Fury and Mick Jagger.

Freddie's later routines led to many questions, eg. did Hitler, whom he regularly impersonated, really wear wellies, along with shorts with swastikas on each knee and during Starr's singing homage to Elvis, another favourite turn, why did he keep breaking off to impersonate a frog? In the 15 years that followed that Royal Variety Performance, little Starr became a big star.

Freddie featured in TV series including Who Do You Do? and Jokers Wild from 1972, later hosting his own show, having had a hit single, It's You, in 1974, before releasing an album, After the Laughter (1989). During the '80s he became one of Britain's highest-paid entertainers, making over £1m / year, having owned Rolls-Royces and racehorses, one of which, Miinnehoma, won the Grand National in 1994.

Starr, like Benny Hill, Jim Davidson and Bernard Manning, was successful with a pre-cerebral, unrepentantly sexist, often racist comedy that became obsolete by the late '80s, due to comedians including Ben Elton, along with shows such as Not the Nine O'Clock News. The impact of his brutal early childhood was cited as explaining the cocktail of neediness and hostility that underscored much of his comedy.

At the Britannia Pier theatre, Great Yarmouth, he coaxed a young woman on stage during 1997, to take part in his routine. "Have you ever felt my balls?" he asked her, as she blushed. "Would you like to feel my balls?" he said, to which she shook her head then he put his hand in his pocket, producing two rubber balls dangling on a rope. It was pure Freddie Starr, being a queasy comedy of embarrassment, in which the audience's hysterical laughter was seen as having veiled fear.

"I had this devilment in me all the time. I asked it to go away, but it wouldn't," he said. His shows became so ramblingly self-indulgent that during the interval of one televised show an executive told him: "You have to focus, Freddie, focus." "What, all of you?" Starr replied. He seemed capable of anything, so that when the Sun splashed with the headline Freddie Starr Ate My Hamster in 1986, the story seemed plausible enough, although it was later disclosed that it had been concocted by Freddie with his agent, Max Clifford, as a practical joke.

His relationship with Clifford soured, like so many in Starr's life, Max later saying: "The only person Freddie Starr has ever loved or cared for is Freddie Starr – Freddie was a nightmare because he had no discipline. He got to the stage, as so many do, where he thought the world revolved around him. He got to be a monster."

Starr said, "Mum was the one that encouraged me into showbusiness. She used to send me off to dance lessons, but I hated it. 'I'm not going,' I'd say. 'There's only girls there.' My dad used to say, 'She's paid half a crown for that lesson, get down there. Aged 15 he appeared in the Liverpool-set film Violent Playground (1958), with David McCallum and Stanley Baker then during the early '60s, he sang for a band titled Howie Casey and the Seniors, which played the Cavern club in Liverpool and toured Hamburg with the Beatles.

Later Freddie sang for a Merseybeat pop group, the Midnighters, put together by Brian Epstein but the relationship with the Beatles manager ended badly. In his autobiography, he stated that Epstein cornered him in a car. "He pushed his face towards mine and tried to kiss me full on the lips ... I didn't send a wreath to his funeral."

Starr wed his childhood sweetheart, Betty Simpson, when he was 17, the couple having had a son, before divorcing after 12 years together. He then wed Sandy Morgan, a dancer in his Blackpool pier show in 1975, the pair having had 3 children before divorcing during 1994. Freddie had an affair with his personal assistant, Julie Dicker, Sandy alleging that their children were so afraid of their father during the marriage that they kept knives under their beds, a claim Starr disputed.

During the protracted divorce Freddie had another relationship, with his one-time manager Trudie Coleman, with whom he had a daughter. He stated in his autobiography that neither of his former wives nor any of his children would talk to him by then. Starr was fined £45 for slapping his son Jody during 1999, saying, "I'm guilty of slapping my lad, but he's also guilty of having a bad attitude and showing disrespect to his father." By 2011 Freddie was repentant, perhaps thinking that he'd visited the sins of his father on his son, stating: "I can see what I've done and I'm very sorry." He wed his secretary, Donna Smith in 1999, with whom he had a daughter, the couple divorcing during 2002 but remarrying a year later.

Starr became a reality TV show recidivist in his later years, attempting to revive a career that had declined to 25 dates / year at smaller British theatres. He appeared on Celebrity Fit Club in 2004 but was demoted as team captain for not taking the show seriously. Freddie made the misguided decision to take part in Celebrity Wife Swap during 2008, he and Donna exchanging with the former page 3 model Samantha Fox and her partner, Myra Stratton. When the programme was broadcast Starr said that the experience had wrecked his marriage, as it made his wife realise how grimly unreconstructed he was, the couple divorcing the following year.

Freddie enrolled as a contestant on I'm a Celebrity ... Get Me Out of Here! in 2011 but in one of the bushtucker trials, he suffered an allergic reaction to the selection of insects and animal parts, including a camel's toe, that he was invited to eat. After hospital treatment he withdrew from the show, returning home to be with his partner, Sophie Lea, whom he wed during 2013.

Starr was arrested by police investigating allegations of historical sexual abuse in 2012 then after spending 18 months on bail, he was told he wouldn't be prosecuted during 2014. The following year Freddie lost a claim for slander and libel against his accuser, who'd alleged that he'd groped her during 1974 when she was a teenager, on the set of the BBC programme Clunk Click, hosted by Jimmy Savile.

Following the high court ruling, which left him facing a massive legal bill, Starr moved to Spain, having told the Mail on Sunday that he hadn't moved "to deliberately get out of paying" having planned to emigrate to the Costa del Sol regardless of the outcome. Freddie was divorced from Sophie in 2015. He was survived by 6 children, Carl, Tara, Stacey, Jody, Donna and Ebony.

It was hard not to think of Alan Partridge when Freddie Starr asked for a meeting at the Holiday Inn just off the M40 near High Wycombe. He'd just been cruelly portrayed in a TV documentary as a vain egomaniac, deserted by his friends and family, a fallen star with an out-of-date act, who couldn't find work anymore, harbouring a grudge about it all. It was tempting to stroll straight past the salesmen at the reception to ask if Mr Partridge, sorry, Mr Starr, was in his room but he arrived from the direction of the car park, looking miserable, announcing that his wife had died last night, which was, of course, a "joke".

He'd periodically reappeared in the tabloids in less light-hearted stories over the 15 years since the hamster eating tall tale: hitting his son, who called the police, having since refused to speak to him, assaulting a Sun reporter, who found him living in a mobile home, with allegations of the the odd 3-in-a-bed romp and even a gay-sex claim. At 57, Freddie's career had ground to a halt, with none of his 4 children, nor his ex-wife or his brother, being on speaking terms with him.

Max Clifford had said in a Channel 4 documentary that none of Starr's former friends wanted to know him anymore, saying: "The only person Freddie Starr has ever loved or cared for is Freddie Starr," which may've explained why he seemed so sorrowful. At first he talked about how people were always telling him that he should be back on the telly, 4.5 million people having watched the Channel 4 documentary:

"That's the sort of pulling power that Freddie Starr has got - I can't help that" but he'd started a petition signed by "thousands and thousands" of his fans to send to C4, complaining that it stitched him up. He discussed his plans for new shows, on TV and in the West End, and of how he was regarded by TV chiefs as a bit of a liability, saying, "I don't think they have much trust in me. People think the TV today is crap. How many physically funny men can walk on stage and not say a word for 10 minutes but get a laugh? Only one person - Freddie Starr."

He railed against Big Brother: "They shag each other, sell the story to the tabloids then fade away. I've been around for 40 years. I must be doing something right to stay at the top. I've mixed with the best: Elvis Presley, Muhammad Ali, Sammy Davis Jnr, Jerry Lewis." His eyes looked glazed beneath the silvery Stringfellow bouffant. "If we were in America now we wouldn't be having this conversation, because they look after their stars."

As Freddie lit another Spanish duty-free cigarette, it was if the red-hot tip had punctured the receptacle for all that pride, the facade beginning to drop as he started talking of his mistakes and how sorry he was for making them. Most of all Starr was sorry for the mess he'd made of his 2nd marriage, neither his ex-wife Sandy, nor their 3 children, having spoken to him for several years. The last time he'd spoken to his son Jody, Freddie had ended up slapping him then spent 9 hours in a police cell.

He was repentant, not having worked for 2 years, saying he was emerging from a 20-year cocoon, due to his addiction to Valium, his speech still being slurred as a result. One of the worst side effects, Starr said, was that it made you feel you were never wrong. "That's a bad thing. You're there to be shot down in flames. When you have a clear mind you can look in the mirror and face your own image. I've done that then I realised my purpose was to make people laugh - that's all."

Freddie could still remember the first time he'd taken Valium. "After 20 minutes, I felt like a weight had been lifted off my mind and I felt balanced. I thought, 'These are good!' but after 3 years, I was destroying myself, destroying my marriage, destroying a lot of things and that was self-inflicted. I hold myself totally responsible. Now I'm clear and I can see what I've done and I'm very sorry."

Alcohol had never been Starr's drug of choice. "I don't drink because I saw my dad drink and my brother drink". Did his father, a bricklayer and bareknuckle fighter in poverty stricken, post-war Liverpool, slap him around when he was drunk? "Never mind slap me, he used to punch me - sometimes spark out." His father died when Freddie was in his teens but in his book he idealised him as a working-class hero, who would use his fists only to defend his honour. He still refused to see him as a violent man. "He was very Victorian but he never picked a fight in his life. He always tried to talk to people first and ask for a word in their ear but if they cornered him, he would let go."

Starr still visited the psychiatrist he'd started seeing after his divorce from Sandy, believing he'd got to know himself better. "Of course, I've been an a*sehole during my life. I'm not a perfect person. I wouldn't dream of doing the things I did in the past. I was totally wrong in slapping my 20-year-old son and I'm sorry I attacked the reporter from The Sun. My behaviour and my attitude have changed drastically. I've realised that life's too short. I can't stand any form of aggravation."

Having become estranged from both sides of his family, his brother also refusing to speak to him, Freddie was hoping for reconciliation. "I think it's time to bury the hatchet as far as my adult children are concerned, and get on speaking terms with them." However, he didn't seem sure of their ages: "Stacey is 17 or something, I think. Donna's about 24 and Jody is 20-odd." He'd apparently forgotten all about his other son, Carl, from his

12-year first marriage to Betty, or his daughter, Tara, 5, from a relationship with ex-manager Trudy Coleman. If Starr failed to resume contact, he said he'd miss giving Donna away when she got married but then said: "I don't know if she's married or not."

Freddie added: "I think it's very important that we reconcile things and get in touch with each other. We don't live for ever. I don't want to regret anything, I don't want them to regret anything and I don't want them to make the same mistakes I did. I'd dearly love to embrace them and hold them then say, 'Don't let's talk about the past, that's gone. Let's look to the future and be friends. That's a bigger priority than my career now."

Freddie Starr groped a 15-year-old girl while she was attending a Jimmy Savile show 41 years earlier, a high court judge found during 2015. Mr Justice Nicol dismissed a claim by the 72-year-old entertainer for slander and libel against Karin Ward, "because her words were true". Starr sued Ward, then 57, over interviews she gave to the BBC and ITV, and statements on a website and in an ebook, in which she said he assaulted her in Savile's dressing room, having called her a "titless wonder".

In May the previous year, the Crown Prosecution Service (CPS) had decided not to go ahead with criminal proceedings against Freddie in relation to allegations by Karin and a further 13 complainants. Sitting at the royal courts of justice in London, Nicol said Ward's account of what had happened was true on the balance of probabilities. "She has proved that it was true that he groped her – an underage schoolgirl – and humiliated her by calling her a 'titless wonder'," he said, in a written judgment.

Dismissing all of Starr's claims, he ordered him to pay Karin's costs, estimated to be close to £1m, which the comedian had to pay on top of his own legal fees. Freddie had told the court the previous month that he didn't at first remember appearing on Savile's BBC show Clunk-Click during March 1974 until footage showed that he was in the studio, with Ward in the audience behind him.

Karin had told the court that Starr, who wasn't present for the ruling, had attempted to give her what was known as "a goose". This occurred when a man "would put his hand under a girl's buttocks to give them a squeeze, usually saying 'goose' and, at the same time, reached for her breasts, saying 'honk, honk,'" she said.

Freddie's behaviour was normal for men at the time, Ward said, but she recoiled because his smell reminded her of her stepfather, who had sexually assaulted her: "I've never complained about it, because it was acceptable at the time. The only thing I complained about was that he called me a 'titless wonder' in a room full of people."

Starr denied the assault, pointing to the fact that the CPS had decided not to prosecute, insisting that it wasn't in his "moral compass" to do such a thing. However, in his evidence, he admitted having a voracious sexual appetite in 1974, having described slapping a girl's bottom during the '70s as "acceptable" behaviour and not sexual. "I'm sorry about the '70s. That's the way it was," he said. Freddie also conceded that he'd made jokes about women's breasts, saying "every man does it", but stated that his humour was "the opposite of humiliation".

Karin was the first of Savile's victims to speak out on camera, with journalists telling the court that her courage had led to 500 other victims of the serial sex attacker coming forward. The mother of 7, a pupil at Duncroft approved school at the time, said she'd performed a sexual act on Savile more than once in return for going to the BBC Television Centre in London for his Clunk-Click show. She was approached by BBC Newsnight in November 2011 after being identified as a victim of Savile from an online book she'd written, in which she referred to him only as "JS".

Ward was at first reluctant to talk, because she was suffering from bowel cancer at the time, but said she agreed under pressure, believing that it would never be broadcast, thinking that she probably wouldn't survive her illness anyway. She also said that she was expressly told that Starr wouldn't be identified. When the Newsnight report was controversially axed, it reinforced her belief that the footage would never see the light of day.

Karin told the court that she had no idea that what she'd written about her life for herself would end up being broadcast worldwide. When she gave an interview to ITV about Savile during October 2012, she said that she again believed that her conversation about Freddie wouldn't be broadcast.

Speaking outside the court after the ruling, Ward said: "It should never have happened. All I can say is: to anybody who hasn't yet come forward who's suffered in the past, don't take this case as a reason not to say anything. Stand tall, it's not your fault. You might not have had a voice years ago, but you have now. Don't give in to bullies."

Her solicitor, Helen Morris, accused the broadcasters of hanging Karin out to dry: "I've never come across a case where a source had been abandoned by a publisher or broadcaster to defend a legal case on their own. It's particularly egregious for the BBC and ITV/ITN to have done so when Karin Ward put her head above the parapet to speak out about Savile."

A BBC spokesperson responded: "We note that Mr Starr himself brought the allegations into the public domain, having sued Ms Ward over various publications, including several reports by ITV naming Mr Starr and online material by Ms Ward which were made before BBC Panorama in October 2012. As a contributor to BBC output, the BBC offered to help Ms Ward with a contribution to her legal costs before the trial and remains willing to discuss a fair contribution to her costs, if these cannot be recovered from Mr Starr as ordered by the court." Freddie had claimed £300,000 in damages for shows he said were cancelled because of Ward's allegations.

27

61

64

69

CPSIA information can be obtained
at www.ICGtesting.com
Printed in the USA
BVHW021457230619
551744BV00014B/543/P

9 780368 804199